THERE IS

PEACE

WITHIN THE

STORM

A Daily Christian Guide to
Recovery Using God's 30-Day Plan

REGGIE YOUNG III

RELENTLESS
PUBLISHING

There Is Peace Within The Storm : A Daily Christian Guide to Recovery Using God's 30-Day Plan

Copyright © 2020 by Reggie Young, III.

Published by :

Relentless Publishing House, LLC

www.relentlesspublishing.com

RELENTLESS
PUBLISHING

ISBN: 9781948829397

First Edition: March 2020

10 9 8 7 6 5 4 3 2 1

Dedication

I would like to thank my family and my beautilful wife, Brandi, for their support. Without you, I would not have the courage to face my fears and walk in my purpose. To my loved ones who I have lost from this disease of addiction and mental health: Titi Nellie, Titi Yolanda, Aunt Ella, Aunt Saundra, Teo Bobby, Teo Louie, Teo Thomas, Uncle Lenny, and Uncle Walt. My cousins Lenny Jr and Julius Young.

To my sons, nephews, and niece, Kyle, Isaiah, Daniel, Christian, Gabriel, Miguel Jr, Amanda, Angel, Andrew Micheal, and Jayden. The generational curse has been broken off your life. I speak prosperity, wisdom, and success over you. You will have a future with love, and happiness. You will have a sound mind and a heart filled with peace and joy. God will watch over you and guide you through the rest of your days. I speak these things over you in the powerful name of Jesus. Amen.

TABLE OF CONTENTS

To the ones reading this book. Always remember….Even Broken Crayons can still color.

There is Peace Within the Storm

Look Away from Yourself

"And Moses made a serpent of brass, and put it upon a pole, and it came to pass, that if a serpent had bitten a man when he beheld the serpent of brass, he lived," Numbers 21:9.

Situations will come into your life that you will be incapable of handling. When you are sick or have a case in court, or your kitchen sink isn't working correctly, you trust the services of professionals, like doctors, lawyers, or technicians, to do them for you. Throughout the period, you depend on their knowledge, skill, and ability to remedy the situation. Even though you don't supervise them, they still will do a fantastic job for you.

The children of Israel were in a similar situation. Their actions against God brought serpents into the camp, which bit many of them to death. They recognized that no matter the problem they faced, God had the power to fix the problem if they could ask for His forgiveness. God instructed Moses to mold a serpent of brass, which was a type of Christ hanging on the cross of Calvary. The dangerous beast instantly left all the people who looked at the statue, and their wounds healed at the same time.

Mental health or addiction of any kind can be as harmful as a snakebite or a scorpion sting. You may have tried all you could, but things are not getting better. The best way to solve a problem is to deal with the source. God, the creator of all things, has the power to take away the confusion in the head and the uncontrollable urge to harm yourself with dangerous habits or substances. You need to listen to God's instructions and do exactly as He commands because obedience always brings blessings.

Prayer: God please give me the strength to be obedient. Renew my mind, heart, and spirit, so I can learn to walk in your favor

Declaration: I declare that I am strong in God. Today I choose to renew my mind because I am made in your image. My heart is yours and I have your Spirit in me. Today I will walk in your grace.

"Where there is Peace there is God"
~ George Herbert ~

3

Notes

Created in God's Image

"So God created man in his own image, in the image of God created he him; male and female created he them," Genesis 1:27.

In the beginning, when God made the first man and woman, He made them resemble Him in many ways. Therefore, humankind has been able to accomplish so much in recent times. Centuries ago, we had no electric cars or mobile devices that could perform so many functions at once just by the click of a button. What humanity can accomplish is a testimony to the power of the Creator behind their existence.

The above examples are only on the physical level. What of the mental, emotional, and spiritual levels? Don't you think it is possible to become more mentally balanced, emotionally stable, and spiritually free from destructive thoughts and habits? Of course, it is possible, and you can achieve it. Those early morning attacks and the late-night struggles can be a thing of the past.

Tell whoever tells you that you are a monster that you are not. Let your neighbors know you can become a better person. The only constant thing is change, and it comes to anyone, regardless of their past. Don't let the ugly stuff you see or hear about yourself get into your heart or head. God didn't create you to live in darkness or a life lower than His original plan.

The Bible says in Mark 9:23, "Jesus said unto him, If thou canst believe, all things are possible to him that believeth." God has made you stronger than you think, and Jesus has given you the answer to your question. God created you in his image, and you have the power to make a decision that can change your entire life now and forever.

Prayer: Father, through Your great grace and immanent presence, I grow every day to become more like You.

Declaration: I declare that through You, I have the power to overcome. I declare that through You I am courageous, and I have the power to change.

"It would barely be necessary to preach dogma if our lives were refections of Jesus. If we were to live like true Christians, there would be no heathens."
~ Pope John XXIII ~

Notes

Some Things Are Not Real

"And they rose up early in the morning, and the sun shone upon the water, and the Moabites saw the water on the other side as red as blood," 2 Kings 3:22.

Your five senses help you to connect with your environment, and you have a mind to help you feel the invisible things around you – things the eyes may not see or the ears hear. This is what makes humans unique creatures of God, supporting the fact that we are all created in the image of God. However, these senses with the mind can deceive you into believing what is not valid. They tell you that you are not going to come out of that problem since you just had another round of that bad stuff this morning. Immediately, you feel defeated, and your mind begins to call you a failure.

In the Bible verse above, the Moabites were deceived by their sight. They woke up to a new day only to allow their senses, instead of what they knew to be accurate, to deceive them. How could so much blood fill a valley without being dried up by the scorching sun or soaking into the ground?

God made you in His image, and that is what He wants you to believe. Your mind and action should focus on how to become free from what is holding you down. Tell yourself each morning that you are not a slave to your problem. Speak to the person you see when you look in a mirror that your struggles are not part of you and must pass one day as you hold firmly to whom God says you are- a free person.

Prayer: Heavenly Father grant me the courage to understand that, through You, I have power.

 Declaration: I declare that through You, I have the power to overcome. I declare that through You I am courageous, and I have the power to overcome.

"Personality is that being that has control over itself "
~ Paul Tillich ~

7

Notes

You Create Your Reality

"For the thing which I greatly feared is come upon me, and that which I was afraid of is come unto me," Job 3:25.

Job was one of the good men recorded in the Bible. He may have had his faults, but the Bible said he lived the best way he could. He had a wife, seven sons, and three beautiful daughters. Everything went well for the Job family until disaster suddenly hit the four corners of his life. All he had was gone even before he could realize what was happening. Who would have thought that one so faultless could fall into difficult and trying times? But our key verse revealed that his mind conceived, incubated, and hatched the problems that came on him and his family.

Having a challenge is one thing, and having hope is another. Struggling with a malfunction in the brain is one thing, and having a positive mindset is another. You cannot hope to come out of your condition if you are always harsh on yourself. It is all right to feel responsible for what you are going through right now, but it is dangerous to live in guilt and blame all your life.

What you say and think of yourself and your condition matters a lot in your effort to overcome your struggles. Unlike Job in the Bible, you need to have a positive mindset, lest something worse sets in. What your mind conceives, it can create, and the negative things you allow in your mind can take on the physical shape to haunt you in life. So, do not let fear or any unhealthy thought occupy your mind. Think positively, and you will have positive outcomes.

Prayer: *Father with renewed faith and forever, O Lord, I step into the future with confidence that only you can give me.*

Declaration: *I declare that today my faith is strong. I step into the future with confidence.*

"The best thing about the future is that it arrives one day at a time."
~ Abraham Lincoln I ~

Notes

Do Not Add to the Problem

"She said, No man, Lord. And Jesus said unto her, Neither do I condemn thee: go and sin no more," John 8:11.

The religious Jews brought a woman of easy virtue to Jesus. Being God himself, Jesus saw that the hearts of her prosecutors were as guilty as hers. In his compassion for the entire human race, he asked those who thought they were perfect to throw the first stones at her. When the crowd could not do it due to conscience, they went away without looking back. This gave Jesus enough time to speak kindly to the woman and tell her to go home and practice positive habits that would help her overcome her unusual urge to do wrong. Unlike the people who wanted her dead, Jesus didn't ridicule her or judge her as many do today. He understood the limitations and fragility of the human race and would never do anything to make things worse.

It is not enough that you feel wrong about your struggle with alcohol, drugs, men or women; you have to do something about those habits. You can continue to give the excuse that old habits die hard while you make little or no effort to stop those bad habits. As Jesus told the accused woman to go and sin no more, likewise, He is telling you that you can stop being a slave to mental health and addiction. He sees in you a free person, one who can make a decision and stand by it. God knows you more than you know yourself, and He is confident that you can wake each morning with joy, peace, and a positive mindset to go about the whole day free from your problems. So, the Lord is saying to you right now, "…Neither do I condemn thee: go and sin no more."

Prayer: Lord Jesus, Governor, and Master of my faith, please help me not to follow my own ways but to wait quietly for Your guidance so that I will walk in a righteous path.

Declaration: Today I kill my fleshly desires. I choose Your way and Your path. Which leads me to righteousness.

"There is a time when we must decide firmly on the direction we wish to take, or otherwise circumstances will make the choice for us. "
~ Herbert V. Prochnov ~

11

Notes

God is on Your Side

"But if ye had known what this meaneth, I will have mercy, and not sacrifice, ye would not have condemned the guiltless," Matthew 12:7.

The political happenings often forced into our face on TV remind us of the need for a clean record to occupy a high office. Candidates from opposing parties do anything possible to dig up the dirty past of their opponents. There seems to be neither forgiveness nor forgetfulness of past deeds. The idea that everyone must pay for every little mistake has taken away pity and kindness from the hearts of millions of patriots. It is good to be loyal and passionate about justice, but when these things give no room for the mercy and grace of God, they destroy instead of building up the people.

As Jesus walked by a field, His hungry disciples grabbed what food they could from the nearest farms. In those days, the poor and hungry were allowed to eat on any farm belonging to an Israelite. This was what the disciples of Jesus did, and because it was on the Sabbath, the angry Pharisees labeled them lawbreakers, guilty of stealing.

People may blame you for being the cause of your predicament. Loved ones may remind you of how you failed to listen to advice and went your way. Doctors may tell you how your past habits caused your present health condition. Everywhere you go, people may do or say things that make you feel bad, but always remember that God is on your side and is willing to show you mercy and give you a fresh start. You don't have to pay to enjoy the forgiveness that comes from God. Accept the mercy He is extending to you and begin a new life in Christ today.

Prayer: *Loving Redeemer, I no longer want to act or treat You like a stranger, but I accept You completely as my Savior and Redeemer.*

Declaration: *I denounce all others and I boldly declare you Lord as my Savior and Redeemer.*

"The Bible is a window in this prison-world through which we can see to eternity."
~ T. Dwight ~

Notes

Walk by Faith: Part 1

"Rejoice evermore. Pray without ceasing. In everything give thanks: for this is the will of God in Christ Jesus concerning you," 1 Thessalonians 5:16-18.

At certain times, you will feel like giving up on life. When you consider what you go through in the hands of people who are supposed to show love and comfort. The horrible sleepless nights due to your trauma, you may be tempted to surrender. In life, there are a thousand and one reasons to give up, to feel discouraged, and to get angry at yourself. But will negative emotions and wrong decisions solve the problem? Do they even look like the best thing to do in such a situation?

Apostle Paul, in his letter to the Thessalonians, expressed his concern for the people who were going through tough times. He started by discouraging them from making decisions that will hurt them or the people who mistreat them. Paul went further to prescribe a better way to handle internal and external crises. He recommended praise and prayer to anyone who wants to rise above personal, mental, and emotional struggles. He had been where they were; therefore, he could relate to the issue quite well.

You don't have to react the same angry way to your condition. Start each new day by thanking God for another opportunity to be alive. Open the window, breathe in air, and imagine the love and power of God filling your heart and mind. Resolve to be grateful throughout the day and avoid thinking or saying negative things at whatever comes your way. Praise will always keep you positive all day.

Prayer: Heavenly Father, You are the greatest example. Come and fill my life and world, so it will reflect Your love.

Declaration: I proclaim that I am love because You are love. My actions words and deeds will reflect and extend love.

> "The world is much more willing to accept the gospel than what Christians are to share it out."
> ~ George W. Peters ~

15

Notes

Walk By Faith: Part 2

"And when Jesus was entered into Capernaum, there came unto him a centurion, beseeching him, and saying, Lord, my servant lieth at home sick of the palsy, grievously tormented. And Jesus said unto him, I will come and heal him. The centurion answered and said, Lord, I am not worthy that thou shouldest come under my roof: but speak the word only, and my servant shall be healed,"
Matthew 8:5-8.

This is one of the stories of faith recorded in the Bible. The faith of the centurion was so strong that Jesus admitted he had the greatest faith in Israel at that time. Why did Jesus say so? The man had a servant who had paralysis. The officer knew Jesus had the power to heal any sickness or disease, but he wanted to have the type of faith that would keep him in victory all the time. So, he recalled how his position in the Roman army gave him authority over dozens of soldiers. He saw Jesus as one who doesn't need to be present to issue commands over the works of the devil or the actions of nature and the environment. This man's strange faith paid off in the end.

You can do better than the centurion can because you have a complete copy of the Bible filled with God's precious and powerful promises. Read and study your Bible and underline all the promises that relate to your condition. Go out with these promises in mind and believe those negative urges or confusion have no power over you any longer. When you text a friend from your mobile device, you have no doubt it will deliver as long as you gave the right instructions. Similarly, when you confess the right scripture, have faith that it will work for you throughout the day and beyond.

Prayer: Father, from today forward, I am determined not to allow my fears to spoil the beauty of my life or to destroy my faith and relationship with You.

Declaration: I claim victory over my fears. I acknowledge the beauty and purpose of my life and in my relationship with You.

"When I look back…. I remember the tale of the old man who said on his deathbed that he had many problems in his life, but that most of them never actually happened ."
~ Winston Churchill ~

Notes

You Have a Part to Play in the Healing Process

"When he had thus spoken, he spat on the ground, and made clay of the spittle, and he anointed the eyes of the blind man with the clay, and said unto him, Go, wash in the pool of Siloam, (which is by interpretation, Sent.) He went his way, therefore, and washed, and came seeing," John 9:6-7.

Many times, we want to have something good without paying a dime. You cannot have everything free all the time. If you do, you may neither know the value nor understand the process through which you obtained those things in the first place. This is why fake high school or college certificates are unacceptable in any sane society. The paper material may be the same, but the sacrifice behind the grades is what is missing. Sacrifice represents the efforts, readiness, willingness, and interest of the bearer to experience positive change.

Heaven is always ready to help those who help themselves. Jesus demonstrated that in the encounter with the blind man. Do not expect God to do the things you ought to do for yourself. In any relationship, each party happily plays its part to keep the atmosphere and environment relaxed and livable. If you want to get over an addiction, begin to avoid things that trigger it. It may be porn sites, friends, internet access, pornographic movies, relaxation spots, or even the smell of those hard drugs. If you suffer from mental health, find out what makes you lose your mind and do all you can to avoid them and make your healing process faster. If the blind man in the Bible did his part and came back completely healed, you too can be free from the years, months, or weeks of mental health or addiction when you play your part well.

Prayer: Heavenly Father, when I open my eyes, grant me the strength to carry out Your holy will and purpose for my life.

Declaration: Father, You are my strength. Today Your will be done. I walk in purpose.

"One person who has learned to master life is better than a thousand who have learned to do it only through the content of the books, but no one can derive something truly worthwhile from life without God."
~ Juniester Eckhart ~

Notes

Jeremiah 2: 1-2

Moreover the word of the Lord came to me, saying, 2 "Go and cry in the hearing of Jerusalem, saying, 'Thus says the Lord: "I remember you, The kindness of your youth, The love of your betrothal, When you went after Me in the wilderness, In a land not sown.

Don't Run Away from God

"For my people have committed two evils; they have forsaken me the fountain of living water, and had hewed them out cisterns, broken cisterns, that cannot hold water. Is Israel a servant? Is he a homeborn slave? Why is he spoiled?" Jeremiah 2:13-14

The problem in humanity started in the Garden of Eden when the devil tempted Eve and stirred up her sinful nature. He did this through a clever line of reasoning. He promised Eve that she would have the knowledge of good and evil. When Eve presented the fruit to Adam, he didn't go consult the wisdom of God even though he knew what he was about to do was wrong but instead he "listened to the voice of his wife". After they ate the fruit, Adam and Eve realized the seriousness of what they have done, and they covered themselves and hid from God.

This singular act brought suffering and death into the world. What they thought would lead to more freedom and control of their own lives led to separation from God. It was a clear example of forsaking and forgetting God.

In our scripture passage, the people of God became bored with God and thought his methods were to slow. They saw how godless nations prospered in their worship of false gods and wanted to be like them. God pleaded with them to come back, but they had no ears to listen any longer. As a loving Father, he warned them that those gods had no power to save. He was sad that those who were born to rule became slaves of their own wrong decisions.

You may have your own remedies, but unless you trust in God and stay with him, you may end up where you started. Don't overcome one addiction, only to get trapped in another one. God's ways are perfect, and if you are willing and patient enough to wait, you will sing a song of victory at last. Decide today to relax in God and refuse Satan's suggestions. Many of his victims have come to realize too late that he is a merciless ruler.

Prayer: Father God, thank you that you are always available in my life that I may experience your love and presence every day for the rest of my life.

Declaration: I will not run. I will rest in your goodness.

"If we remain alert and vigilant, God reveals Himself continuously to us and we will rejoice in everything that happens to us."
~Jean Pierre de Caussade ~

Notes

2 Corinthians 5:5

For we know that if our earthly house, this tent, is destroyed, we have a building from God, a house not made with hands, eternal in the heavens.

Your Past Does Not Define Who You Are

"Therefore if any be in Christ, he is a new creature: old things are passed away; behold all things have become new," 2 Corinthians 5:17.

When you come to God through Jesus Christ, the sins you committed in the past are washed away. Your old nature of disobedience and rebellion is taken away, and you stand before God righteous and blameless. The devil or your conscience has no authority to accuse you or make you feel guilty again. But you need to study the word of God to know more about how the new life works. Lack of knowledge of who you are and what you have in Christ will give room for your past to haunt you.

It is not easy to believe you are free when you just had another wrap of those harmful substances. It is difficult to claim your freedom when you still feel yourself losing your mind. Once you follow the Bible's way of approaching God through confession of sins and the mistakes of the past, invite Christ into your life and believe the Holy Spirit is living inside you. It is not abnormal to feel guilty or think the whole repentance stuff is not working. You should expect to have some doubts about the salvation of your soul.

The best weapons against doubts at that point are prayer and studying the word of God. The Christian life is described as a life of faith, and until you believe you have it, you cannot have it. You may struggle with those symptoms but keep believing. You may find yourself drawn to porn or drugs once in a while but don't quit believing you are saved. You have the responsibility of removing all the things that tempt but give God room to bring to manifestation the new life He has given you.

Prayer: Father, thank you that, by confessing my sins to You, I experience Your merciful and loving forgiveness and therefore live and learn to forgive myself.

Declaration: I confess that I am a sinner. I rejoice because I am forgiven. You have shown me mercy and kindness, so today I extend mercy and kindness to others.

"For him who confesses his guilt the pretense is past and the reality has begun."
~William James ~

Notes

Fight to the End

"Fight the good fight of faith, lay hold on eternal life, whereunto thou art also called, and hast professed a good profession before many witnesses," 1 Timothy 6:12.

Apostle Paul was addressing Timothy on the need to remain focused and persevere to the end. He knew the young pastor might be overwhelmed by the enormous tasks in his hands. Paul did not hesitate to let him know that it takes a lot of courage to deal with matters of life and death. The destiny of the souls of the members of the Church was in the hands of Timothy, and he could not afford the luxury of being the cause of their eternal damnation. He worked hard day and night, fighting off laziness, carelessness, and childishness to make sure that none of his actions or inactions would be the reason for any failure.

It is cowardice to look for an easy way out of a problem that needs confrontation. The world is fast becoming a place filled with luxury goods, and many people are buying the idea of a stress-free and comfortable life. The washing machine does the laundry, and we can switch on or off household appliances from a distance. People of past centuries would envy our accomplishments if they were alive today. Yet, this is not an excuse to take what comes to you less seriously. In life, only the courageous will stand in the face of challenges. Determine to go through that therapy or visit the counselor regularly until all the symptoms are no more. No day should pass without reading and praying the word of God. Always hope for daily victory and expect no less by the end of the day. Your battle is not over until it is truly over.

Prayer: Lord, help me to be human with a backbone in an environment full of hurt and ambition.

Declaration: Today I will walk courageously. With You by my side, I will have no fear or worries. I will put everything in your hands.

"Our greatest glory is not in never falling, but in rising every time we fall."
~ ConFucius ~

Notes

One Step at a Time

"Surely I would take it upon my shoulder, and bind it as a crown to me. I would declare unto him the number of my steps; as a prince would I go near unto him," Job 31:36-37.

The journey of a thousand miles begins with one step. No matter how important a project is, a single step is what it takes to get started. Life is a marathon; you run with patience and reserve some energy because you know the finish line is still a long way off. People who ignore this important rule bring their lives to an abrupt and painful end. They forget that, as an African proverb says, " *Patience is the medicine of the challenges of life.*"

In the book of Job, we come face-to-face with the suffering that Job passed through in life. He did not know what he did to deserve the myriad of troubles that came upon him. His friends, who should have comforted him, blamed him for his woes. But Job was not the man easily moved by negative talk. He found courage in his efforts to take one step at a time until he was out of his problem. He was so bold that, if God had asked him what steps he had made to alleviate his problems, he was ready to give a definite answer.

Like Job, have you tried something towards recovery, solution, or improvement? Did you take your medication this morning before going to work? Do you still see your counselor or doctor regularly? These are the little steps you need to consider as you trust God for complete and perfect healing sooner or later. One step at a time is a sure way to get to where you are going faster. No excuse should come between you and your efforts to get back to normal. The more you fail to do something today, the further you delay your chance of getting out of your condition.

Prayer: *Father, I come to You asking humbly to give me strength for one more step and one more after that. Keep me connected to You because You are the vine that gives me life.*

Declaration: *You have ordered my steps. I am one step closer to healing and restoration. I choose to stay connected to You because You are the vine that gives me life.*

"No one can achieve their dreams and become the kind of person they were meant to be all at once. It's a series of little movements, and you can only take the step that's right in front of you."
~ Josh Hatcher~

Notes

1 Peter 3: 8-9

Finally, all of you be of one mind, having compassion for one another; love as brothers, be tenderhearted, be courteous; 9 not returning evil for evil or reviling for reviling, but on the contrary blessing, knowing that you were called to this, that you may inherit a blessing.

Do the Right Things

"For he that will love life, and see good days, let him refrain his tongue from evil, and his lips that they speak no guile: Let him eschew evil, and do good; let him seek peace and ensue it. And who is he that will harm you, if ye be followers of that which is good?" 1 Peter 3:10,11,13

Life is for the living, and the living is for life. This is one thing that should never get out of your mind when you wake each morning. The portion of the Bible for today is an encouragement to do the right and proper things. Most often, we forget that our being good and kind has little to do with the other person. The kinder you are, the better you become and the faster your body and mind heal. To know this fact is to enjoy a good life and good health for the rest of your life, for nothing can compare with peace of mind.

People may call you out in public or whisper to one another as you walk on the streets. You may hear stories about you that never happened, and some may move you to react. This is entirely normal, and you can do nothing to stop people from talking. Responding in anger will do no good. It only makes matters worse, and you may end up hating yourself more for the way you acted. Focus on working on yourself and allow the new life to speak for you. There is nothing that can shut people's mouths faster than clear evidence of success. Concentrate your efforts on improving your life and getting the needed spiritual and professional help, and God will announce your recovery in His own time.

Prayer: *Most Precious Father, I pray each day that You pour Your love into my heart, so I may live only as You want me to live, and I make the choices You only want me to make.*

Declaration: *Today God I choose You; I choose life over death. I choose joy over sorrow. I will do what you deem to be right*

"Do the right thing. It will gratify some people and astonish the rest."
~ Mark Twain ~

Notes

Confide in Someone You Trust

"Confess your faults one to another, and pray one for another, that ye may be healed. The effectual fervent prayer of a righteous man availeth much," James 5:16.

Rumor mongers will always exist in every human society, and the advent of technology makes news travel faster. This is an indication that there is nothing you can do once the words leave your lips into the ears of the other person. The only way to keep essential issues to yourself is either to tell no one about it or tell only the people you trust. Some problems in our lives are meant to be shared to find solutions, comfort, sympathy, or whatever response we expect. There are problems that, once we share them, we experience instant and surprising peace in our hearts.

The Bible tells us of the need to share our problems with people who are in the position to offer quality help. These people may be your parents, older siblings, pastor, doctor, or counselor. The roles these persons play make them deserving of our respect and trust. If they happen to be righteous people, they can join hands with you in prayer to God for speedy healing. It is not a good thing to bottle up an issue that is eating you up mentally, emotionally, and physically. Look for someone you can confide in and pour out your heart until those things hurt no more.

There is power in unity, and you can try it and see. Jesus promised to answer the prayer made by two or more people concerning any matter. Take advantage of this promise and draw closer to full recovery and healing. Good things are always worth trying if you want to begin a life free from unnecessary mental and emotional suffering.

Prayer: Loving Father, allow my heart to be humbled that I might share my heart's burden with the people You placed in my life.

Declaration: Fear has no power over me. I am not bound by my past. In my testimony lies freedom.

"We rarely confide in those who are better than we are."
~ Albert Camus ~

Notes

God is Stronger than Your Condition

"And I give them eternal life, and they shall never perish, neither shall any man pluck them out of my hand. My Father, which gave them me, is greater than all; and no man is able to pluck them out of my Father's hand. I and my Father are one," John 10:28-30.

According to a story, all members of a snake family crossed dense and dangerous forests to attend an important snake meeting. It was dark when the session ended, and the group had to return home that night. Thinking of the scary things in the way, the little snakes looked up at their mother and asked in fear, "Don't you think some dangerous animals will harm us on the way?" Mother snake laughed and then with a sober look replied, "What could be more dangerous than a snake, my dear ones," she said.

In our text, Jesus was telling the people of the power of God, but it seemed they do not want to listen. Little wonder only a few disciples followed the Lord at that time until Pentecost. Jesus painted the picture of how dear believers are to God. No spirit or human condition can do away with what God holds in His hands. That is why, as a believer, you should never worry about tomorrow as long as you are doing what is right day and night, in secret and in the open. The Bible is a book that shows who you are and what you have in God through Jesus Christ. It is either you take God at His word or go ahead worrying over your physical or mental condition. God is working behind the curtains through His word to release you from that condition. When God is invited into your matter, nothing can stand in His way, not even terminal illnesses.

Prayer: *Father, You are the Alpha and Omega. You are a miracle-working God. Guide me to Your word, which gives me refuge from my enemies.*

Declaration: *God I invite You into my situation. You are Alpha and Omega. You are The Great I Am. I am expecting a miracle of complete recovery. I thank You in advance.*

"Fight your battles through prayer and win your battles through faith."
~ Luffina Lourduraj ~

Notes

Rise Quickly When You Fall

"Rejoice not against me, O mine enemy: when I fall, I shall arise; when I sit in darkness, the Lord shall be a light unto me. I will bear the indignation of the Lord because I have sinned against him, until he pleads my cause, and execute judgment for me: he will bring me forth to the light, and I shall behold his righteousness," Micah 7:8.

Prophet Micah was one of the strongest advocates of the mercy and power of God. His book is replete with comments that highlight his unshakable faith in the benevolence and love of God for His creatures. Here, he seemed to turn his attention to people who laughed at the fall of someone sincere and struggling with the challenges of life. Micah boldly told them to watch how God's mercy flows deep down to pull up those who have been battered and broken by wrong choices. He expressed hope for the future and was sure that unfavorable conditions have an end.

You will have days when you feel like men and God have abandoned you. Sometimes the loneliness will be so painful that you begin to lose hope in getting out of your problems. Those are not the moments to feel dejected; God is interested in your wellbeing, and He is always there for you. Your actions or wrong decisions may have put you in the mess that you are in right now. God's mercy and grace can break through any barrier to reach the biggest of sinners. So, you can count on God for the strength to stand on your feet and move on with Him. Stop brooding over past mistakes but rise and accept the mercy and grace that God extends to His creatures each new day.

Prayer: *Father God, You call everyone who is tired and overburdened to You. Lord, I graciously accept Your invitation with humility and praise.*

Declaration: *Out of the darkness I rise. I rise from the brink of despair. I stand tall and faithful to your guidance. Condemnation I place you under my feet. You don't control my mind anymore. I am an overcomer*

"How else but through a broken heart can Christ enter a life?"
~ Oscar Wilde ~

Notes

Keep Your Eyes on the Reward

"Brethren, I count not myself to have apprehended: but this one thing I do, forgetting those things which are behind, and reaching forth unto those things which are before, I press toward the mark for the prize of the high calling of God in Christ Jesus," Philippians 3:13-14.

Paul the apostle was a man who, more than anyone in his time, understood what Christianity was all about. Although he persecuted the Church, after his conversion, he became a powerful instrument for the spread of the gospel. God revealed to him profound truths, and Paul didn't hesitate to share some of that knowledge with fellow Christians. His struggles with the flesh and the spirit taught him valuable lessons, which he passed on to believers today. He never allowed the things he suffered to move his eyes away from the purpose of His calling. Today, when you talk about victorious and exemplary saints of old, Paul the apostle stands out as bright as the sun.

Here is a lesson you should never forget if you want to see to the end of anything you are working on. The decision to seek help and begin the process of healing is a good one. People and circumstances will try to make you feel unloved and irredeemable. You need to have a strong backbone to stand on what you believe until you have achieved your aim. No good thing has ever been accomplished without a fight. If you keep listening to your five senses and feeling like those symptoms are still there, you lose your focus. As long as you are doing everything possible to get out of the mess, do not allow any negative thought to occupy your mind.

Prayer: Risen King, I place my life and well-being in your faithful care, and I step into the unknown future with strength and confidence.

Declaration: With strength and confidence I declare my future will be greater than my past. I will keep my focus on You God. I am a warrior and Your word is my weapon.

"For the Christian, the final heartbeat is not the conclusion of a meaningless existence, rather it is the glorious beginning of a life that will never end."
~ James Dobson ~

Notes

Light at the End of the Tunnel

"For there is the hope of a tree if it is cut down, that it will sprout again, and that the tender branch thereof will not cease. Though the root thereof wax old in the earth, and the stock thereof die in the ground; Yet through the scent of water, it will bud, and bring forth boughs like a plant," Job 14:7-9.

Job's friends heard of his suffering and visited him. After sympathizing with him, they rolled out a thousand and one reason Job deserved such a measure of suffering and affliction. They reminded him that no wicked person could escape the consequences of their action. But Job knew he was innocent of any crime and did not deserve to be in that condition. He told his friends he believed that one day, his sufferings would be over. And Job was right; his troubles came to an end when God visited him and blessed him with more than he had previously.

Your sufferings also will be over if you think and act like Job. From the time you were born to this very point in your life, you have known that no condition, no matter how terrible, lasts forever. When you are suffering pain or dealing with some serious diseases, it is often difficult to remember important facts about life. No matter how dark the night, there will be a break of dawn. No matter how heavy the storm, it will pass, and the sun will shine again. Even the hungry soul will end up finding a kindhearted stranger to feed them. So, always keep hope alive, for that is what cannot be taken from you when everything else fails.

Prayer: *Lord Father, seal me as your faithful servant and keep me in Your bosom for eternal life.*

Declaration: *Today I will not worry about things that are out of my control, but I will have faith in God because I know He is Master of all things.*

"The minute you settle for less than you deserve you get even less than what you settled for."
~ Maureen Dowd ~

Notes

Better Late Than Never

"They say if a man put away his wife, and she goes from him, and become another man's, shall he return unto her again? Shall not that land be greatly polluted? But thou hast played the harlot with many lovers; yet return unto me, saith the Lord," Jeremiah 3:1.

Marriage is the only relationship that God expects us to keep sacred until the end of our lives. It is a relationship so sensitive that a little lie or unfaithfulness can destroy what had taken years to build. God wants His children to respect marriage vows and to find common grounds to stay together. Sometimes, a severe case of adultery can threaten marriage, and both parties will call it quits. Due to the nature of the wrong decisions of the offending partner, it may be difficult for both parties to remain together. But God is saying that He is willing to welcome back anyone who was separated from Him by a life of crime, drugs, or wrong choices.

Every one of us has made mistakes one way or another. You don't have to spend your entire life regretting your past actions or forever blaming yourself. Yes, you might have picked up a bad habit the day you repeatedly visited a website and fed your mind with pornographic pictures. Your love for puffs of smoke or strong drinks might have plunged you into your current struggles with mental health or addictions. Whatever it may be or however long you have been in your condition, God is telling you that it is not too late to return to Him in repentance and faith. He is always willing to receive those who come to Him for a new life. Return to God now and delay no longer.

Prayer: Lord, thank You for Your mercy. Father looks beyond what I am and inspire me to be what You know I can be. Let me never hide behind my fears or trauma.

Declaration: I will not hide behind my fears or trauma. I take hold of this opportunity for a new beginning. I choose to start today and be an inspiration for others.

"It is never too late to be what you might have been."
~ George Eliot ~

Notes

Look to the Future Not the Past

"Remember ye, not the former things, neither consider the things of old. Behold, I will do a new thing; now it shall spring forth; shall ye not know it? I will even make a way in the wilderness, and rivers in the desert," Isaiah 43:18-19.

When you were a kid, you probably were scared when you noticed your shadow for the first time. That dark patch followed you, walked and ran with you wherever you went. You tried to outsmart it by suddenly running off, but there it was, stuck to you and would never let go. Our past, especially when riddled with mistakes and wrong choices, is like a shadow. It trails us, lurks in the dark, and remains shrouded in mystery. You may be helpless when it comes to a real shadow, but your past shouldn't be allowed to haunt you forever.

God, through Prophet Isaiah, is speaking to you now about your past. He is saying that you have allowed your history to stop you for a long time. You have never let go of the hurts, the regrets, and the self-blame. You still hold them tightly like your blanket on cold nights. His assurance to you is coming at the right time. You may have suffered severe trauma, but He is telling you to forget the past and focus on the future. God has a better plan for you, even if you are not proud of your past. A clean and promising future is what we all have in common. Break free from the past, consciously live in the present, and hope to enjoy the future. God is telling you so, and you know He never lies. Congratulations, in advance, on your bright, pure, and great future.

Prayer: Lord God, draw near to me. I need You now. Let my heart be changed and my mind renewed by The wonderful love I found within You.

Declaration: I forgive me, I love me, I am a gift from God. I have a new heart and a renewed mindset. I can do this!

"Do not let the shadows of your past darken the doorstep of your future. Forgive and forget. "
~ unknown ~

Notes

Mind Your Thoughts and Language: Part 1

"Out of the same mouth proceedeth blessing and cursing. My brethren, these things ought not so to be. Doth a fountain send forth at the same place sweet water and bitter? Can the fig tree, my brethren, bear olive berries? Either a vine, figs? So can no fountain both yield salt water and fresh," James 3:10-12.

The Bible warns against idle words or what we call today's negative words. The language people use today has made it difficult to notice when negative statements escape our lips. The pop culture, violent movies, and gangsters' slang have flooded the minds of people with ideas that do not glorify God or edify humankind. The moment you try to eradicate one bad language, another one comes up and begins to reign among the young and old. It is becoming apparent that the world is under the grip of foul language. Only true believers are secure through constant meditation on God's word.

In the book of James, we discover that negativity is not the only possibility. It is also possible to live both in the positive and the negative at the same time. The Bible compares that possibility to a stream that produces salt and fresh water, which is not naturally expected to happen. It is so when you, a perfect creation of God, allow negative thoughts about your condition to prevail in your mind. Who told you that you cannot come out of that mental state to live a healthy and sane life? Who said you cannot be free from drugs, porn, cocaine, or marijuana? Those negative thoughts are not from God; they are from your mind or Satan. You win when you mind your thoughts and language. Be a person with positive thinking!

Prayer: Loving God gives me the wisdom to choose my thoughts and words carefully and always to speak with love in my heart.

Declaration: I repent of every negative thing I have spoken about myself and my situation.

"Don't always say what you want to say unless you want to hear what you would not like to hear."
~ Seamus MacManus ~

Notes

Mind Your Thoughts and Language: Part 2

"We had the same spirit of faith, according to as it is written, I believed, and therefore have not spoken; we also believe, and therefore speak; Knowing that he which raised up the Lord Jesus shall raise us up also by Jesus, and shall present us with you," 2 Corinthians 4:13-14.

The day you became a new creature, God gave you the Holy Spirit to live in your heart. The Spirit comes in with great blessings, one of which is faith in the heart of the receiver. This faith by the Spirit of Faith is ever able to carry you through tough times. God's gift of the Spirit is the evidence of a possible future resurrection, healing, deliverance, and miracles in your life. When God raised Jesus from the dead, he was demonstrating his power in the lives of all those who believe and accept Jesus Christ as their personal Lord and Savior.

You have more than you think you have to be complete in life. God's promises in the Bible weren't made for angels; they were made for humans. The blessings written in Genesis down to Revelation are for you. Confess them with your mouth and believe them in your heart. Mention them in prayers and carry them in your thoughts throughout the day. Speak them when you face challenges and stand on them when those demons come to trouble your mind.

There is power in thoughts and language filled with the positivity that comes from the knowledge of God's word. Sometimes, ordinary positive thinking, conjured by mental energy, is ineffective. You need to have God's thought in your mind and use God's language in your words when you confront your problems or face the enemies of your soul each day as you move towards recovery and complete healing.

Prayer: Holy Father, let the words I speak be pleasing in Your sight and sweet melodies to Your ears.

Declaration: Today I will speak and think positively, so it can be manifested in the flesh

"Hold on to the words of God that you hear with your ears because they are nourishment for the soul."
~ Pope Gregory 1 ~

Notes

Be Thankful For Life

"And Hannah prayed, and said, My heart rejoiceth in the Lord, mine horn is exalted in the Lord: my mouth is enlarged over mine enemies; because I rejoice in thy salvation," 1 Samuel 2:1.

Hannah's prayer serves as an example of the problem people encounter in many parts of the world today. She was barren for many years, in spite of the love her husband had for her. Since her husband had two wives, the second woman would mock her condition, and Hannah would cry her heart out all day and all night. She wanted to have a child and feel the pride of motherhood that some women crave. At last, her prayers were answered, and Hannah went to the temple and made a prayer of thanksgiving to the Lord Almighty.

Like Hannah, you should learn to thank God at all times, no matter the condition you face. Being grateful is a quality many people lack today. It is something that attracts blessings from God and men and creates a positive attitude in you. Don't allow your situation or medical condition to make you bitter about life. If you look around you and observe, you will see the need to be thankful to God. In the program of God, you don't have to wait for something good to happen before you praise the name of the Lord. Hannah was of the Old Covenant; you are of the New Covenant and need to walk by faith. Thank God for life itself and praise His name for making you see another day. Being alive is a form of assurance that you have another day to expect healing, recovery, and the blessings of peace of mind. Learn to thank God by faith every day of your life.

Prayer: "Heavenly Father, I thank You for the everyday things You provide for me in my life and for everything they mean to me.

Declaration: I am extremely grateful for what I have and what is yet to come. I will rejoice in the present.

"Learn to be thankful for what you already have, while you pursue all that you want."
~ Jim Rohn ~

Notes

Count Your Blessings Not Your Losses

"My brethren, count it all joy when ye fall into diverse temptations; knowing this, that the trying of your faith worketh patience. But let this patience have her perfect work, that ye may be perfect and entire, wanting nothing," James 1:2-4.

Temptations and trials come to everyone on earth, regardless of status, gender or country of residence. As believers, we are admonished to take everything that comes to us in good faith and not gets infuriated by it. We may feel like we suffer more than all the people in the universe, that our problems are unprecedented and our troubles never experienced by any living being. We fail to see the blessings behind everything we go through. Our sad experiences make us wiser and better. Without the unpleasant experiences of life, we may never possess our current level of knowledge.

No matter what you go through, understand that someone somewhere is having a harder time than you. Somebody in Asia or Africa has no access to a mental institution or a qualified counselor. In most countries of the world, survival is a game for the rich and well-connected. The poor and less privileged have nothing and no one to run to for help. Despite what you feel you don't have, you have something someone somewhere is begging to have. As each day dawns, some people have less reason to stay alive, but they still try to keep hope alive. They cherish the little they have and trust God for something better in the future. With their poor health and weak mind, they still count their blessings and not their losses. Adopt this attitude and watch how your problems grow painless and less tenacious. When God says count your blessings, he has a big surprise up his sleeve.

Prayer: God, thank you for your grace, mercy, and everlasting favor.

Declaration: Today I am grateful for everything that is provided to me. The losses in my life are nothing but lessons that I have overcame

"It is impossible to lose everything and still be alive."
~ Mokokoma Mokhonoana ~

Notes

Evil Thrives in the Dark

"And this is the condemnation, that light comes into the world, and men love darkness rather than light because their deeds were evil. For every one that doeth evil hateth the light, neither cometh to the light, lest his deeds should be reproved. But he that doeth truth cometh to the light, that his deed may be manifest, that they are wrought in God," John 3:19-20.

Jesus Christ knew the heart of men and the motive behind every action. In his night discussion with Nicodemus, He told him about the new birth and the blessing of being a child of God. He made him understand that, without total deliverance from a life of darkness, no human can be genuinely saved. Darkness is a term used to represent Satan, sin, and the secrecy surrounding sinful actions in the world. Jesus knew that people often hide their true identity, their real character, and their true intentions. Sin is shameful, so those who commit it don't want to be caught red-handed.

Whatever shameful, displeaseing or umcomfortable situation you are facing today may have come through a sin committed in the past. Sin has been the problem God has had with humankind since the world began. You are not condemned because you committed a crime. You are doomed for rejecting the way of salvation that God brings through Jesus. The sin committed secretly and the love for secret sins will be the major hindrance to full recovery. The devil rejoices when you keep to that bad habit because he knows he will continue to have power over you as long as you are living in darkness. Abuse of drugs, pornography, masturbation, and infidelity are some of the dark acts that keep men away from God and His Light. Leave the dark and come to the Light today.

Prayer: Lord, I accept the truth that the new life will be full of temptations. Help me lead a victorious life with the weapon of the Holy Spirit.

Declaration: I will let the Holy Spirit guide me so I can continue to walk in God's favor.

"There are good and bad times, but our mood changes more often than
our fortune."
~ Thomas Carlyle~

59

Notes

Satan is the Real Enemy: Part 1

"Be sober, be vigilant; because the adversary the devil, as a roaring lion, walketh about, seeking whom he may devour: who resist steadfastly in the faith, knowing that the same afflictions are accomplished in your brethren that are in the world," 1 Peter 5:8-9.

The battle humankind faces go beyond the physical realm. The scarcity of food, financial troubles, mental health, drug addiction, and several other battles are just manifestations of what has gone wrong in the spiritual realm. Satan is the cause of the sufferings in this fallen world, and he continues to be the chief architect of the sufferings of the sons and daughters of men. He plans to terminate God's perfect will for all flesh and establish a world of chaos, disorder, and untold hardships. But we are commanded by God to resist him by our faith in God's promises until we overcome.

In the real sense, no mortal on earth is your enemy. Satan is behind the actions of men and women. What you are currently struggling with is caused by Satan, but with your permission. Satan knows he cannot achieve his aim without your cooperation. He tries to get your attention and then sells you his wares. That is why, before you begin to blame yourself or the people who introduced you to a wild lifestyle, first you have to battle and overthrow Satan. Only then will you have the freedom to experience the fullness of God's blessings.

Prayer: Lord God, Captain of my heart and soul, Satan knows I follow You. Guard my heart, Lord God, so that it beats for You alone.

Declaration: I declare that God has a plan for my life, and Stan you are no longer in control.

"Real men laugh at opposition; real men smile when enemies appear."
~ Marcus Garvey

Notes

Satan Is the Real Enemy: Part 2

"So the servants of the householder came and said unto him, Sir, didst thou not sow good seed in thy field? From whence then hath it tares? He said unto them, An enemy hath done this. The servants said unto him, Wilt thou then that we go and gather them up?" Matthew 13:27-28.

The above verse is from a parable told by Jesus to demonstrate what will happen on the final day. It also illustrates what happens in life until the time of the end. In the world, we have good people, bad people, kind people, mean people, humble people, and horrible people. Even God himself allows evil people to live to see if they will change before their end comes. That is why the man in the story suggested the wheat and tares grow together until the harvest. The reason is that the devil is the real enemy of all humankind. Behind every evil man or woman, boy or girl, old or young, is the devil.

While God wants you to take responsibility, he also wants you to know the truth. God created human beings in a way that makes them submit to either God or the devil. There is never a time you are free from God or Satan. Those days you did what you liked and cared less of God, you were under the chains of the devil. It is the devil who put you in the mess that you are in right now. He may have used your mind, your loved ones, or your friends to destroy your future. The truth is that Satan is the one who tempts people to do bad things. Fight off the devil, so that evil and evil people will stay away from you.

Prayer: *Almighty loving GOD, cover my mind with Your powerful helmet of salvation; remind me that I am Your child. Change my thoughts, God, on what is true, honorable, right, and pure in your eyes.*

Declaration: *I declare that I have a sound mind filled with good thoughts and I will no longer walk in defeat but in triumph.*

"Forgive your enemies, but never forget their names."
~ John F Kennedy ~

Notes

Run When You Should

"Do this now, my son, and deliver thyself, when thou art come into the hand of thy friend; go, humble thyself, and make sure thy friend. Give not sleep to thine eyes, nor slumber to thine eyelids. Deliver thyself as a roe from the hand of the hunter, and as a bird from the hand of the fowler," Proverbs 6:3-5.

The Book of Proverbs contains a lot of wise instructions to guide the ways of the wise and prudent. Here, the preacher advises anyone who wants to avoid regrets to do all they can to save themselves from the many traps of the wicked. Satan and his agents are out there, waging war against the good and righteous. Those who will overcome are those who will not rest until they are free from all the suggestions and actions of evil. Just as the roe or the bird struggles to break free from traps, the Book of Proverbs admonishes us to make efforts to stay safe and sound.

Life itself is a risk, and every day you expose yourself to risks of different kinds and various levels. There are some kinds of risks that you must never take in life. Doing so will invite the worst mistakes and regrets imaginable. If you are experimenting with a new and dangerous drug, stop it before it becomes too late to stop. If you are already in a mess, don't do it anymore. Seek help and begin the process of healing. It is better late than never in your case. Don't let your mind deceive you that, since you are already into it, there is nothing you can do but continue and probably die in it. The Book of Proverbs is suggesting to you the best way to be free from addiction.

Prayer: Father, help me to tie the belt of truth around my waist and have the Holy Spirit guide my thoughts to discern what is the truth from lies.

Declaration: I run away from evil, and walk toward Your mercy and love.

"Most people never run far enough on their first wind to find out they've got a second."
~ William James ~

65

Notes

Never Walk Alone

"I will instruct thee and teach thee in the way which thou shalt go: I will guide thee with mine eye. Be ye not as the horse, or as the mule, which hast no understanding: whose mouth must be held in with bit and bridle, lest they come near unto thee," Psalm 32:8-9.

God is a loving God, and King David knew this better than anyone in his time. David probably remembered how he started as a shepherd boy and ended up a king in the palace. His was a typical story of Grass to Grace. He knew that, without God, he couldn't have reached the heights he attained. When he slept with Uriah's wife, he suddenly knew it was dangerous to walk alone, without God and without his word to guide him every day. Walking with God was the only way to stop avoidable problems from coming near him.

Do you have the same story to tell? Have you made a big mistake that you could have avoided if you were more careful? Are the problems you are going through a result of not walking with God? Are you about to make a decision out of anger and frustration without consulting God first? These critical questions may go on, but the essential thing is that, unless you walk with God, you cannot hope to have a happy ending. Walking alone may have its attractions, but the benefits of walking with God far outweigh them. Look at what your lack of obedience to God in the past has cost you. Surrender your life to God today by accepting Jesus as your personal Lord and Savior. Only then can you begin a real walk with God that has benefits now and in eternity.

Prayer: Father, I am encouraged in You. You said that You will always be with us. I know You have and always will be fighting for me. I thank You for Your love and Your promises.

Declaration: I declare I am never alone as long as I have God in my heart. With You in my life Father, I will never be alone again.

"If you make friends with yourself, you will never be alone. "
~Maxwell Maltz ~

Notes

About the Author

A native of Brooklyn, New York, Reggie Young has overcome much adversity in life to stand where he is today. Both sides of his family suffered from drug abuse and mental illness, forming the foundations of what he would later become. Rather than giving in, Reggie graduated high school and joined the Navy. There he earned a Bachelor of Arts in Computer Info Systems and set course for a career in IT.

Ask any veteran and they will tell you how difficult it is to transition from military to civilian life. Reggie was no different, struggling with a bout of alcohol-related issues stemming from PTSD. It was then he realized he needed a change. He started a nonprofit called House of Stars and Stripes and dedicated his time, money, and energy to helping homeless veterans find employment, housing, and the proper training for a new career.

Reggie graduated with a degree in Social Work from Liberty University and is currently working on his Master's Degree in Social Work from LSU. He credits faith for helping pull him back from the edge and knows it can do the same for everyone else. To learn more about his incredible story or House of Stars and Stripes, you can follow Reggie at **www.houseofstarsandstripes.com**

Resources

https://suicidepreventionlifeline.org/

https://www.mentalhealth.va.gov/suicide_prevention/veterans-crisis-line.asp

https://www.usa.gov/food-help

https://www.auntbertha.com/

https://www.hudexchange.info/housing-and-homeless-assistance/

https://www.kinf.org/programs/srs/

https://www.assurancewireless.com/partner/freshebt

https://www.ed.gov/

https://www.va.gov/

www.ingramcontent.com/pod-product-compliance
Lightning Source LLC
Chambersburg PA
CBHW060350050426
42449CB00011B/2910